Extreme Places
The Oldest and the Newest

KATIE MARSICO

Children's Press®
An Imprint of Scholastic Inc.

Content Consultant
Injeong Jo, PhD
Assistant Professor
Department of Geography
Texas State University
San Marcos, Texas

Library of Congress Cataloging-in-Publication Data
Marsico, Katie, 1980– author.
The oldest and the newest / by Katie Marsico.
    pages cm. — (A true book)
 Summary: "Learn all about the oldest and newest places on Earth and find out how the world has changed over time." — Provided by publisher.
 Includes bibliographical references and index.
 ISBN 978-0-531-21846-4 (library binding : alk. paper) — ISBN 978-0-531-21785-6 (pbk. : alk. paper)
1. Antiquities—Juvenile literature. 2. Trees—Age determination—Juvenile literature. 3. Volcanic eruptions—Juvenile literature. 4. Barnenez Cairn (France)—Juvenile literature. I. Title. II. Series: True book.
CC76.M37 2016
902—dc23   2015012579

All rights reserved. Published in 2016 by Children's Press, an imprint of Scholastic Inc.
Printed in the United States of America 113
SCHOLASTIC, CHILDREN'S PRESS, A TRUE BOOK™, and associated logos are trademarks and/or registered trademarks of Scholastic Inc.
1 2 3 4 5 6 7 8 9 10 R 25 24 23 22 21 20 19 18 17 16

Front cover (main): The Ta Prohm temple in Cambodia

Front cover (inset): Nishinoshima Island

Back cover: Scientists brushing dirt from the mummy of a child

Find the Truth!

Everything you are about to read is true *except* for one of the sentences on this page.

Which one is **TRUE**?

T or F   New islands formed by volcanic ash usually last forever.

T or F   Certain types of trees can clone themselves.

Find the answers in this book.

Contents

1 An Endless Blend of Old and New

How do the old and the new
together shape life on Earth? **7**

2 Exploring an Ancient Burial Site

What do archaeologists know about one of
the world's oldest surviving structures? **13**

3 The Birth of an Island

What causes new islands to form,
and how long do they last? **21**

THE **BIG** TRUTH!

Surviving the Test of Time

What are some of Earth's
oldest organisms? **26**

Ginkgo leaves

People in South Sudan celebrate their country's independence in 2011.

4 Timeless Trees

How do some trees manage to survive thousands of years?

. . . . 29

5 A Brand-New Nation

How was the new country of South Sudan born?

. . . 37

True Statistics 44

Resources 45

Important Words 46

Index 47

About the Author 48

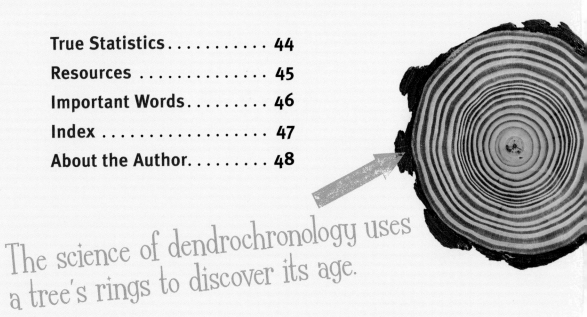

The science of dendrochronology uses a tree's rings to discover its age.

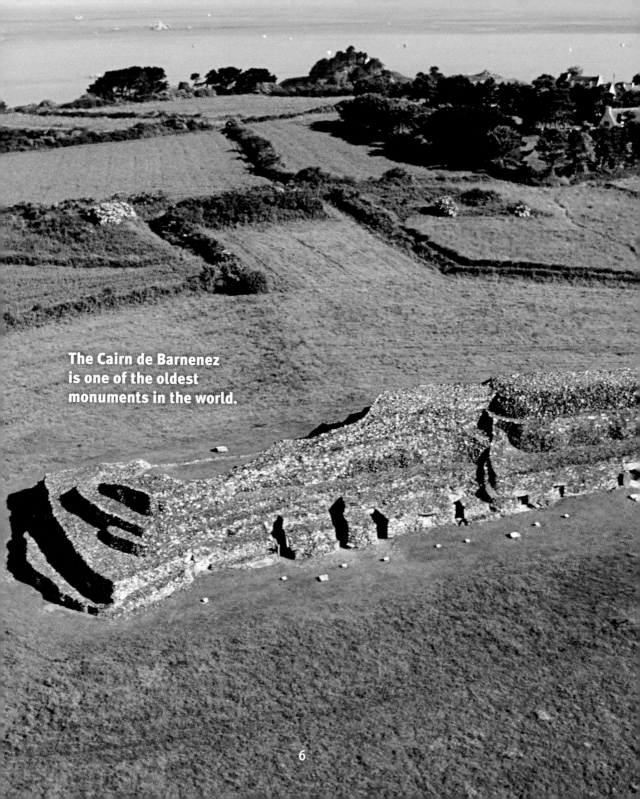

The Cairn de Barnenez is one of the oldest monuments in the world.

An Endless Blend of Old and New

An imposing stone structure winds along the northern coast of Brittany, a region in northwestern France. Located on a steep hill, it overlooks the sea. This structure is one of the world's oldest burial sites. Parts of it were built in 4500 BCE. This makes Barnenez older even than the Egyptian pyramids.

A cairn is a pile of stones that marks an important place.

Continuity and Constant Change

Our world is constantly changing. Some changes occur rapidly. A new island or a new country may be established almost overnight. At the same time, some aspects of life on Earth show remarkable continuity. A single tree may live through countless human generations, or a structure, such as the Cairn de Barnenez, may stand for several thousand years. All these elements shape our lives, forcing us to **adapt** to what is new while tying us to the past.

This image of daily life appears on a box found in the ancient city of Ur, in what is now Iraq. The city was first settled around 3,000 BCE.

Volcanic activity under the sea can give rise to brand-new islands above the waves.

Earth has existed for billions of years. In that time, a number of forces, both natural and human, have shaped the planet. Natural forces may be biological—connected to plants and animals—or **geological**, such as earth-shaping landforms. Human forces may be cultural, driving the creation of monuments and cities, or **geopolitical**, shaping countries and their governments. Although humans have been around for only a fraction of Earth's existence, their impact on the planet is enormous.

Talking About Time

People describe the passage of time in a number of different ways. The term *prehistoric* refers to the period before anyone kept written records. *Ancient* describes the distant past. In contrast, the word *modern* refers to the present or the recent past.

The calendar that most of the world uses today expresses dates in terms of the Common **Era** (CE) or Before the Common Era (BCE).

Earth's Story: A Timeline

4.6 billion years ago
The planet Earth forms.

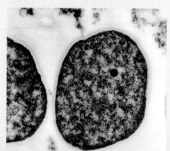

3.8 billion years ago
Single-celled organisms appear on Earth.

The year traditionally believed to be the year of the birth of Jesus, the central figure of the Christian religion, is counted as year 1 of the Common Era.

Taking note of time helps us understand our relationship to the past and to the future. Whether it's an awe-inspiring ancient monument or a new nation born of political ideals, both the old and the new play a role in creating our world.

200 million years ago
Earth's single large landmass starts splitting into smaller continents.

200,000 years ago
Human beings first walk on Earth.

4500 BCE
What scholars consider the earliest city, Uruk, is built in what is now the Middle East.

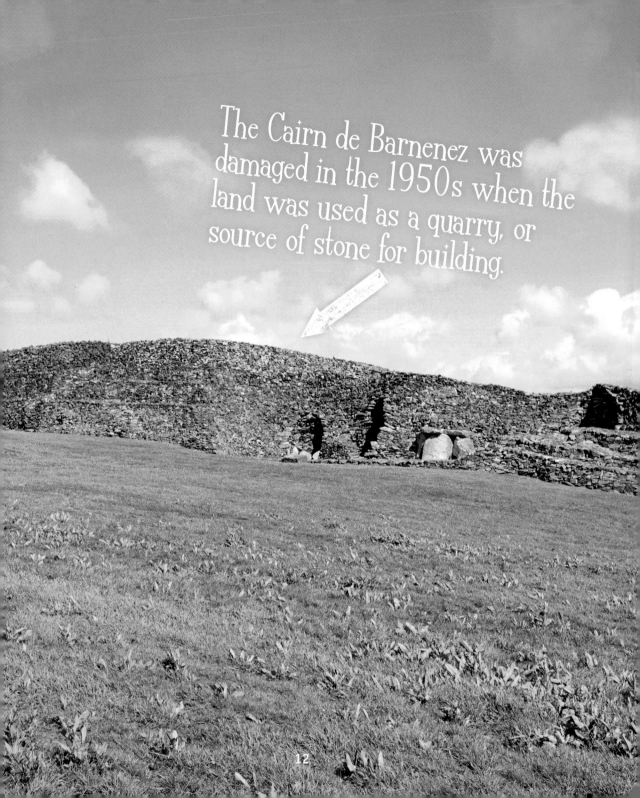

The Cairn de Barnenez was damaged in the 1950s when the land was used as a quarry, or source of stone for building.

CHAPTER 2

Exploring an Ancient Burial Site

About sixty years ago, workers digging for stones to build a road uncovered the ancient tombs of the Cairn de Barnenez. Lost to time and covered with grass, this **mausoleum** housed eleven ancient tombs. The building measures 246 feet (75 meters) long. At its widest point, Barnenez stretches 92 feet (28 m) across. It is Europe's largest stone mausoleum and was built in two stages, about 300 years apart.

Cairn de Barnenez

How Old Is Old?

Archaeologists believe Barnenez is one of the oldest buildings in the world. They reached this conclusion using a process called radiocarbon dating. Carbon is an element present in most of Earth's organisms. A small amount of carbon is radioactive. This means that it produces a powerful energy known as radiation. When an organism dies, the radioactive carbon in its body remains there until the organism **decomposes**.

A scientist prepares a sample for carbon dating.

14

Any material that was once part of a living thing can be carbon dated, including bone.

If the organism's body hardens into a fossil, the radioactive carbon doesn't immediately disappear. Eventually, it begins to decay. Archaeologists know the rate at which such decay occurs. By studying the amount of decay in a fossil's radioactive carbon, scientists can tell how long an organism has been dead. The process of radiocarbon dating therefore helps them estimate when the organism died.

The tombs at the Cairn de Barnenez are passage tombs, entered through a narrow passage that leads to the burial chamber.

Footprints of the Past

Carbon dating of burial materials at Barnenez has shown that the tombs date back more than 6,500 years to about 4500 BCE. **Artifacts** such as pottery, axes, and arrowheads also help researchers piece together information about the people who built the mausoleum. Other clues to its history include symbols and drawings etched onto Barnenez's stone walls.

Archaeologists suspect that the people who constructed the mausoleum started out as hunter-gatherers. It's likely that, over time, they settled in the area and began farming there.

Today, portions of Barnenez are open to the public. While extremely old, the stone structure has endured. It serves as the lasting footprint of an ancient civilization.

Many people travel to the French region of Brittany to see the Cairn de Barnenez.

Religious Ruins

Some historic ruins are ancient burial places. Others are temples built for religious worship. In Mexico, Belize, Guatemala, and Honduras, they often reflect the religious practices of the early Maya people. More than 2,000 years ago, the ancient Maya constructed elaborate stepped temples throughout Mexico and Central America. Archaeologists believe they used these structures to worship their gods. The Maya may also have used them to study the sun, moon, and stars.

The Maya city of Palenque in what is now Chiapas, Mexico, contains a number of temples, tombs, and other structures.

Ancient Wonders

Many ancient civilizations have left their footprint in the modern world. Like Barnenez de Cairn, the famous pyramids of Egypt are ancient monuments that were built as mausoleums. These burial chambers housed the remains of early Egyptian rulers called pharaohs. The largest pyramid, the Great Pyramid at Giza, dates back to about 2600 BCE. It was built with 2.3 million limestone blocks—some of which weigh up to 16 tons!

Great Pyramid

This new island in the Pacific grew quickly, eventually colliding with a nearby island.

The island nation of Tonga includes more than 170 islands in the Pacific.

20

CHAPTER 3

The Birth of an Island

Since its formation, Earth has continued to change and grow. Early on, geological events such as earthquakes and volcanic eruptions brought about the creation of continents and oceans. Even today, new geographic landforms are reshaping Earth's surface. For example, a new island emerged in the Pacific Ocean as recently as January 2015.

♀Tonga Archipelago

The new island arose between these two islands, both part of Tonga.

A Fleeting Formation

In December 2014, an underwater volcano erupted in the South Pacific. The volcano, named Hunga Tonga-Hunga Ha'apai, is part the Tonga **archipelago**, a chain of islands in the South Pacific. The volcano lies about 40 miles (64 kilometers) north of the nation's capital city, Nuku'alofa. As the eruption progressed, large amounts of ash began pouring out of the volcano. By January 2015, so much ash had piled up from the underwater eruption that a new island rose up from the sea.

People first noticed the new island in a satellite image taken on January 19, 2015. By that point, the mound of ash had risen above the surface of the water. Experts measured it to be nearly 1.3 miles (2 km) long and 1 mile (1.5 km) wide. Most of the landscape, composed of volcanic ash, is blackish gray.

Hunga Tonga-Hunga Ha'apai's eruption of ash blotted out the light from the shoreline.

The island features an emerald-green lake. However, it's not likely that many people will want to swim in it. The lake smells strongly of sulfur, which often produces a powerful odor like that of rotten eggs. Sulfur is one of the chemicals frequently released during volcanic eruptions. Yet even if visitors could stand the stench, the island's desolate landscape of ash makes it both unwelcoming and possibly short-lived.

Lakes containing sulfur are often found around volcanoes. This one is located in the Kuril Islands between Russia and Japan.

This island is the top of the Stromboli Volcano, which formed thousands of years ago off the coast of Sicily.

Some volcanic islands are formed when hot, molten rock flows from volcanoes as lava, which hardens over time. While lava can create fairly stable islands, an island made mainly of ash can more easily wash away in the water. It's impossible to predict exactly how long such islands will last. In the meantime, however, scientists continue to explore the newest addition to the Pacific.

Surviving the Test of Time

Some animal and plant species have survived on Earth for so long that they form a living bridge between prehistory and the present. Their stories provide a glimpse into Earth's earliest plant and animal life. They also help lead scientists to a better understanding of modern species.

A Glance at Ginkgoes
Many experts consider ginkgoes to be the oldest trees on Earth. Some ginkgo fossils trace back roughly 270 million years! Several adaptations may have helped the trees last so long, including insect-resistant wood and the ability to sprout new trees from growths on the branches of old trees.

Hardy Horseshoe Crabs

Horseshoe crabs have earned the nickname "living fossils." These animals predate even the dinosaurs! Some horseshoe crab fossils date to approximately 450 million years ago. Horseshoe crabs may have survived thanks to an extremely effective immune system.

An Ancient Flower

Amborella trichopoda doesn't look tough. This South Pacific shrub has evergreen leaves and tiny white or yellow flowers. But *Amborella* has endured for 130 million years. Recognized as one of the oldest flowering plants, it's extremely valuable to scientists. Researchers hope to learn more about modern petal-bearing plants and their prehistoric ancestors by studying *Amborella*.

Prehistoric Predators

Scientists believe sharks first appeared between 455 million and 425 million years ago. Some now-extinct sharks and modern shark species even lived at the same time. For example, Megalodons, which disappeared 1.6 million years ago, and great white sharks, which live today, once swam together in ancient oceans.

Old Tjikko stands only 13 feet (4 meters) tall.

CHAPTER 4

Timeless Trees

At first glance, Old Tjikko doesn't look particularly stunning. In fact, many observers may simply mistake the Norwegian spruce for a scraggly Christmas tree. Yet there's far more to Old Tjikko than meets the eye. This particular spruce is believed to be the oldest living plant on Earth. After studying its roots, scientists believe the tree is roughly 9,500 years old!

Fulufjället National Park

Forests cover about one-third of Fulufjället National Park.

A Long-Surviving Spruce

Old Tjikko is located in Fulufjället National Park in central Sweden. Scientists first noticed the spruce while conducting a study of trees in the area in 2004. The visible parts of Old Tjikko—including its trunk and branches—are not especially old. But as scientists eventually discovered, the tree's root structure dates back thousands of years.

Researchers took samples of Old Tjikko's roots to analyze them more closely in a laboratory in Miami, Florida. Scientists there used radiocarbon dating to estimate the tree's age. Based on what they learned, they declared Old Tjikko to be the world's "longest-lived plant." And after approximately 9,500 years on Earth, the tree is still growing!

Scientists have to study the chemical makeup of a Norwegian spruce's roots to learn its age.

Scientists determined that Old Tjikko has survived so long because it can clone itself. In other words, the spruce is able to independently replicate, or copy, certain cells. Whenever Old Tjikko's trunk dies, new cells form and, over time, grow a new trunk in its place. This is an especially useful adaptation because the spruce's trunk typically lasts no more than 600 years.

This great gray owl perches on a Norwegian spruce as it watches and listens for prey.

Ancient bristlecone pine trees like these grow in the mountains of California.

An Aged Pine

Old Tjikko is just one of many trees that are known to be several thousand years old. Not all of these trees have the ability to clone themselves. A bristlecone pine named Methuselah does not possess this adaptation. However, it has still managed to endure for almost 5,000 years! Methuselah is located in Inyo National Forest in California's White Mountains.

Tree rings are layers of wood that grow around a tree's core trunk.

Scientists figured out Methuselah's age by counting its tree rings. In some trees, such as pines, new rings grow every year. This helps people know the lifespan of a particular tree. Using this method, scientists proved that Methuselah and other bristlecone pines existed for an extremely long time. These trees have several features that have made such a long life possible.

One of the pine's adaptations is a system of far-spreading roots that absorb hard-to-reach moisture. A second is wood that appears resistant to damage caused by insects, rot, and disease. Yet one danger still threatens these ancient trees—humans. For this reason, park rangers often don't reveal the trees' precise locations. They keep such information secret to prevent the trees from being cut down or **vandalized**.

Methuselah is one of many bristlecone pines in Inyo National Forest.

South Sudan's national flag was originally designed in the 1990s and used by people who fought for the country's independence.

CHAPTER 5

A Brand-New Nation

Not unlike volcanic eruptions that change Earth's physical landscape, political movements can sometimes lead to abrupt and dramatic change in the world. The birth of the world's newest nation, the Republic of South Sudan, in July 2011, is an example of such rapid change in the geopolitical landscape. Before then, it had been part of a larger North African nation called the Republic of Sudan.

South Sudan

South Sudan has a population of 11.5 million people.

Separating From Sudan

For decades leading up to July 2011, the Sudanese people were entrenched in two violent civil wars. Experts point to a range of reasons behind this unrest. These include religious and **ethnic** differences between citizens in northern and southern Sudan. Another cause involved disagreements over ownership of resources such as oil, water, and farmland.

Decades of conflict in Sudan resulted in millions of deaths from violence or starvation. Millions more people fled their homes as refugees.

Activists chant, hold signs, and wave flags in support of South Sudan's independence leading up to the referendum vote.

At various times in their history, people in Sudan's southern region, called South Sudan, had been allowed to govern themselves. Ultimately, however, fighting continued to erupt between northern and southern forces. Then in 2009, leaders from both sides of the conflict agreed to hold a special referendum. A referendum is a public vote on a single political question or issue.

Voting on South Sudan's independence took place over the course of a week.

In this case, Sudanese citizens would decide whether South Sudan should be granted complete independence. In turn, the leader of Sudan, President Omar al-Bashir, agreed to accept the results of the referendum. In January 2011, the Sudanese people cast their votes. Almost 99 percent of them supported South Sudan's total freedom from Sudanese authority. So, on July 9, 2011, South Sudan was declared an independent nation.

The World's Youngest Countries*

The following are the world's 10 newest nations. A nation is a geographical area with its own, independent government.

Flag	Country	Date of Birth	Former Identity
	The Republic of South Sudan	July 9, 2011	Part of the Republic of Sudan
	The Republic of Kosovo	February 17, 2008	Part of the Republic of Serbia
	The Republic of Serbia	June 5, 2006	Part of the State Union of Serbia and Montenegro
	The Republic of Montenegro	June 3, 2006	Part of the State Union of Serbia and Montenegro
	The Democratic Republic of Timor-Leste	May 20, 2002	Part of the Republic of Indonesia
	The Republic of Palau	October 1, 1994	Part of the United Nations (UN) Trust Territory of the Pacific Islands
	The State of Eritrea	April 27, 1993	Part of the Federal Democratic Republic of Ethiopia
	The Czech Republic	January 1, 1993	Part of Czechoslovakia
	The Slovak Republic/Slovakia	January 1, 1993	Part of Czechoslovakia
	The Republic of Bosnia and Herzegovina	March 3, 1992	Part of the Socialist Federal Republic of Yugoslavia

*As of 2015

Like many other new nations, South Sudan's future is far from certain. As it grows and develops, the country continues to experience conflict. There is still tension between the Sudanese and South Sudanese. In addition, different ethnic groups within South Sudan don't always get along. Poverty and hunger are serious and widespread problems that the South Sudanese must address.

Tens of thousands of people, displaced by years of war, currently live in refugee camps across South Sudan.

Thousands of people visit the Maya ruins at Tulum, Mexico, each year.

Amazing Extremes

From the fledgling nation of Southern Sudan to the newest island in the Pacific, the world is constantly changing. Meanwhile, some things—from sturdy trees to ancient monuments—endure. Change and endurance together shape life on our planet. Even as we remain tied to the past, something new will always be around the corner. ★

Earliest date that portions of the Cairn de Barnenez were constructed: 4500 BCE

Amount of time between the construction of Barnenez and the construction of the Egyptian pyramids: About 2,000 years

When ancient Mayas began constructing temples: More than 2,000 years ago

Year a volcanic eruption caused the formation of a South Pacific island: January 2015

Age of Earth's longest-lived plant (Old Tjikko): Approximately 9,500 years

Age of the bristlecone pine named Methuselah: Almost 5,000 years

Date that South Sudan formally declared its independence from Sudan: July 9, 2011

Did you find the truth?

F New islands formed by volcanic ash usually last forever.

T Certain types of trees can clone themselves.

Resources

Books

Maloy, Jackie. *The Ancient Maya*. New York: Children's Press, 2010.

Masters, Nancy Robinson. *Volcanic Eruptions*. Ann Arbor, MI: Cherry Lake Publishing, 2012.

Owings, Lisa. *South Sudan*. Minneapolis: Bellwether Media, 2012.

Putnam, James. *Pyramid*. New York: DK Publishing, 2011.

Visit this Scholastic Web site for more information on oldest and newest places:
★ www.factsfornow.scholastic.com
Enter the keywords **Oldest and Newest**

Important Words

adapt (uh-DAPT) — to change over time to fit in better with the environment

archaeologists (ar-kee-AH-luh-jists) — people who study the material remains of past human cultures and activities in order to learn about the past

archipelago (ahr-kuh-PEL-uh-goh) — a group of islands

artifacts (AHR-tuh-fakts) — objects made by human beings, such as tools or weapons used in the past

decomposes (dee-kuhm-POZE-iz) — rots or decays

era (ER-uh) — a long period of time in history that has some consistent feature

ethnic (ETH-nik) — of or having to do with a group of people sharing the same national origins, language, religious beliefs, or culture

geological (jee-uh-LAH-ji-kuhl) — related to Earth's physical structures, especially its layers of soil and rock

geopolitical (jee-oh-puh-LIH-tih-kul) — of or having to do with geographical, economical, or social factors that influence the government

mausoleum (maw-suh-LEE-uhm) — a building that contains a tomb or tombs for burial of the dead

vandalized (VAN-duh-lyezd) — deliberately damaged or destroyed

Index

Page numbers in **bold** indicate illustrations.

adaptations, 26–27, 32, 35
Amborella trichopoda, **27**
archaeologists, 14, 15, 17, 18
artifacts, **16**

al-Bashira, Omar, 40
Before the Common Era (bce), 10–11
Belize, 18
bristlecone pine trees, **33**–35

Cairn de Barnénez, **6**, 7, 8, **12**, **13**, 14, 16,
    17, **43**
calendar, 10–11
civil wars, 38
cloning, 32, 33, 34
Common Era (ce), 10–11

earthquakes, 21
Egyptian pyramids, 7, **18**, **19**

fossils, 15
Fulufjället National Park, **29**, **30**

geological activity, 21
ginkgo trees, **26**
Great Pyramid at Giza, **18**, **19**
Guatemala, 18

Honduras, 18
horseshoe crabs, **27**
Hunga Tonga-Hunga Ha'apai, 22, **23**
hunter-gatherers, 17

Inyo National Forest, 33

lava, 25

Maya people, **18**
Methuselah tree, **33**–35
Mexico, 18

Old Tjikko tree, **28**, **29**, 30–32

radiocarbon dating, **14**–**15**, 31
referendums, **39**–40
refugees, **38**, **42**
roots, 29, 30, **31**, 35

sharks, 13, **27**
South Sudan, **36**, **37**, 38–**40**, 41, **42**
sulfur lakes, **24**

timeline, **10**–**11**
Tonga, **20**, 22
tourism, **17**, **24**, **43**
tree rings, **34**

volcanic eruptions, 21, **22**–**25**

About the Author

Katie Marsico graduated from Northwestern University and worked as an editor in reference publishing before she began writing in 2006. Since that time, she has published more than 200 titles for children and young adults. One day, Ms. Marsico would love to visit both the Cairn de Barnenez and the Egyptian pyramids.